Gareth Southgate!
Annual

ALWAYS 100% UNOFFICIAL

Adam G Goodwin

Dicken Goodwin

Jonathan Parkyn

Gareth Southgate! Annual

First published in the United Kingdom in 2018 by

Portico
43 Great Ormond Street
London
WC1N 3HZ

An imprint of Pavilion Books Company Ltd
Copyright © Pavilion Books Company Ltd 2018
Text copyright © Yes/No Publishing Services 2018

ISBN 978-1-91162-223-9

A CIP catalogue record for this book is available from the British Library.

10 9 8 7 6 5 4 3 2 1

Reproduction by Rival Colour Ltd, UK

Printed and bound by G. Canale & C. S.p.A., Italy

This book can be ordered direct from the publisher at
www.pavilionbooks.com

THIS BOOK BELONGS TO

6

WRITE YOUR NAME ON THE SHIRT AND JOIN MY TEAM!

Contents!

Contents!

Welcome!

...Gareth Fans!

Wowsers! What a fab year for fans of the England men's football soccer team, and what a stupendous year for the country's new favourite son, Gareth Southgate. Like a slowly emerging phoenix from the flames, Gareth has risen from the pain of a crucial penalty miss in Euro 96, to the giddy heights of steering the rookie England team to the semi-finals of 2018's football soccer world cup! Equipped with his super-smart waistcoat, hipster beard and 'new man(ager)' sensibilities, the G-man has cut a swathe through the 'old school' culture at football soccer's highest level. We love you, Gaffer Gareth!

Inside 'The Unofficial Gareth Southgate Annual' you will find a bulging sack of Gareth Southgate-shaped footballs for your enjoyment. Featuring glorious games such as *The Great Gareth Hunt*, *Gareth's Spot the Balls*, *Pin the Waistcoat on the Gareth*, and not only, but also including the super exciting stories *Southgate Holmes and the Case of the Speckled Ball*, *Gareth and His Amazing Technicolour Waistcoat* and the photostory *The Penalties of Love* starring a young Tony Hadley from top pop band Spandau Ballet as the young Gareth. With hunky poster pics, fashion and personal grooming tips, horoscopes, recipes, mazes and puzzles aplenty, there is enough Gareth-infused fun to keep all the family entertained through to Euro 2020, Qatar 2022 and beyond!

The Editor

SOUTHGATE'S
NATIONAL TREASURES

Treasury XI

COLLECT 'EM!

SWAP 'EM!

SNIFF 'EM!

GARETH **SOUTHGATE**
MANAGER

100% APPROVED

SPEED	78
CHARISMA	88
POWER	66
HUGS	95

NT INDEX **90**

100 FOOTBALL SKILLZ

FLICK 'EM!

STICK 'EM!

SPEND LOADS OF MONEY ON 'EM!

IT'S OFFICIAL! OUR GARETH IS A NATIONAL TREASURE!! THEN WHO BETTER THAN 'SUPER SOUTHGATE' TO PUT TOGETHER A SUPREME TEAM OF NATIONAL TREASURES TO COMPETE IN THE NATIONAL TREASURES WORLD CUP, IF IT EXISTED? COLLECT THE STICKERS AND SEE WHO HAS MADE THE SQUAD (EVEN THOUGH IT DOESN'T EXIST).

STICKY-STICKERS, STICKY COLLECTABLE, STICKER-BOOK ADHESIVE FUN!!

GARETH'S BLATTER SPLATTER GAME

Oh no! In a bid to take over FIFA, exiled Sepp Blatter has cloned himself many times over using insect DNA to create an unbeatable swarm of mosquito Blatters to spread disease across the footballing world!

PEST CONTROL

PEST CONTROL

Chief Mosquito Swatter Southgate has heroically captured the original Blatter, but can you help him splatter the remaining Blatters with your 'Blatter Splatter' mosi swatter?

MOSQUITO SWATTER

Hidden throughout the following pages of this annual are a further eleven buzzing Blatters. Find them and circle them, then return to Gareth here with the page numbers where they were discovered.

I, Deputy Mosquito Swatter ....
hereby pledge my allegiance in the fight against the disease that the cloned Sepp Blatter mosquito team are attempting to spread across the footballing world.

The eleven Blatter mosquitoes were splatted on

Page Page Page Page

Page Page Page Page

Page Page

Page

Southgate's SPOT THE BALLS Game

Gareth has decided that this game of Spot the Ball is far too easy. Look – it's just above that Swedish player's head. So, to make the puzzle more challenging, Gareth has hidden loads of other balls in the picture.

CAN YOU FIND AND IDENTIFY ALL GARETH'S BALLS?

- ☐ Meatball
- ☐ Prawn Ball
- ☐ Pokeball
- ☐ Snowball
- ☐ Ballpoint Pen
- ☐ Ball of Wool
- ☐ Dough Ball
- ☐ Zoe Ball
- ☐ Ballcock

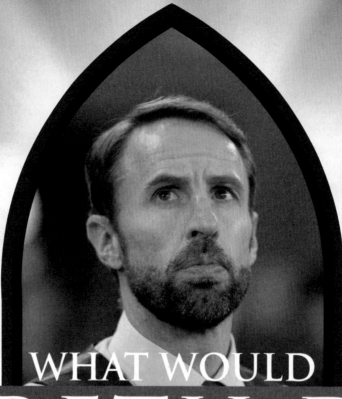

WHAT WOULD GARETH DO?

As England's coach, Gareth Southgate seems to have solutions for all the nation's footballing woes. But how would he solve people's everyday problems? Here's some of the brilliant advice that Gareth might offer if he was a famous agony uncle instead of a famous footballer slash England manager.

A BRUSH WITH LOVE

Dear Gareth...

I think I'm in love with a girl at work. She's called Sinead and she has lovely brown hair and amazing shoulders. But how do I make her notice me? I've tried leaving her gifts – a bottle of her favourite shampoo and also some Chewits (strawberry). I really like her. Sometimes when I see her brushing her hair, I imagine I am her hair being brushed by her hairbrush! I've tried catching her eye, but I think she might be short-sighted, because she just avoids my gaze or runs away. Please help!

Steve-o (32) Banbury

WHAT GARETH MIGHT SAY...

Love does not choose its victims, Steve-o. But when love strikes, it scores. Be honest. Be virtuous. And open your soul to Sinead, so that she, in turn, may open hers to you. Also, if she's not into Chewits, maybe consider inviting her to Pizza Hut? There's a great 2-for-1 deal on at the moment.

WE CAN WORK IT OUT

Dear Gareth…

I've got a problem at work. Usually, I achieve my goals, especially under stress. But ever since I've joined this new team, I've been struggling to hit my targets. I'm really good with my colleagues and I help them out whenever I can. But I just can't seem to close a deal and I'm worried that my new boss is going to sack me. He's a nice guy and has been supportive so far, but he is starting to get criticised for my performance.

Raheem (23) Manchester

WHAT GARETH MIGHT SAY…

Success is an elusive creature, Raheem. It tempts us and goads us on, and then slips though our fingers, like the grain we scatter in our pastures. But remember – to not succeed is not to fail. Be patient. Bide your time. Continue to work hard. Success will inevitably arrive. Besides, you've got ages till Euro 2020, anyway.

THE 'SWEAT' SMELL OF SUCCESS

Dear Gareth…

I don't know if you can help me but I have a big problem with excessive sweating. I sweat from everywhere: my armpits, my palms, my lumbar region and so on. Anywhere that has skin, basically. My mum says it's normal, but she would say that. She's a heavy sweater, too! It's really getting me down. It makes me so sad, that sometimes I even sweat from my eyes!

Macy (14) Midlothian

WHAT GARETH MIGHT SAY…

Don't be ashamed of your sweat, Macy. Embrace it. Perspiration is an indicator of dedication, endeavour and toil. Wear it like an emblem of your strength and goodness. Alternatively, try wearing a waistcoat – they're great for hiding all manner of stains and secretions.

JEALOUS GUY

Dear Gareth…

I recently lost my job and now the new guy who took over is absolutely smashing it. He's handsome, wears a fancy waistcoat, and has never once been investigated for alleged corruption. I am well-jel and can't stop thinking angry thoughts. Can you help?

Sam A (64) By text

WHAT GARETH MIGHT SAY…

If jealousy is a sin then we are all sinners, Sam. And if anger is invading your thoughts, then why not try channelling that negative energy into positive deeds and thoughts? You could give a sad-looking stranger a hug, perhaps? Just don't let any undercover reporters film you doing it!

1950s
The Sir Stanley

1960s
The Sir Bobby

1970s
The Keegan

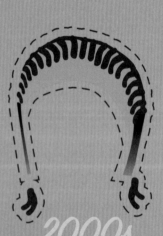

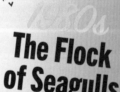

1980s
The Flock of Seagulls

1990s
The Fresh Prince

2000s
The Beckham Braid

2010s
The Marcelo

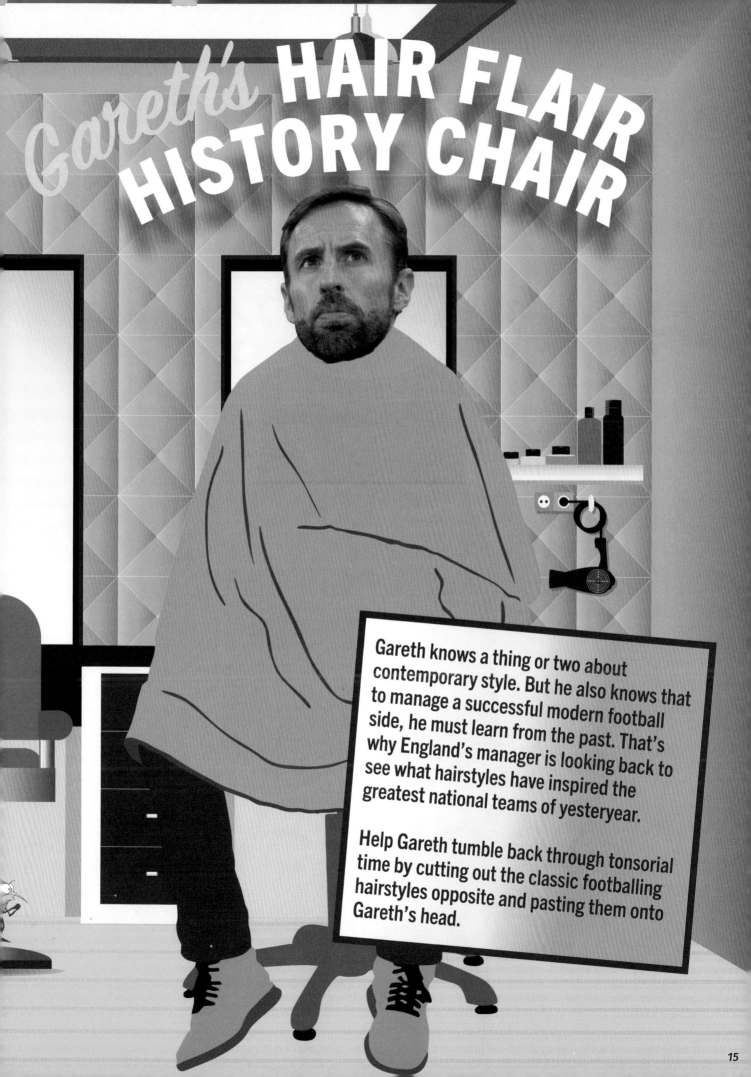

Gareth's HAIR FLAIR HISTORY CHAIR

Gareth knows a thing or two about contemporary style. But he also knows that to manage a successful modern football side, he must learn from the past. That's why England's manager is looking back to see what hairstyles have inspired the greatest national teams of yesteryear.

Help Gareth tumble back through tonsorial time by cutting out the classic footballing hairstyles opposite and pasting them onto Gareth's head.

Gareth
and the
Amazing
Technicolour
Waistcoat

Way, way back, many centuries ago in the 1990s in the holy land of Wembley, it came to pass that there was then living a young man named Gareth Southgate, who was one of eleven brothers that did toil together in England's football fields, under the controversial leadership of Terry Venables. And thus it was that Gareth did speak much more poshly than his brethren and had O levels. And his brothers were jealous of his poshness and they did taunt him upon the clarity of his speech, calling him 'Nord', for it was that he did sound most like Denis Norden, the ancient presenter of *It'll Be Alright on the Night*. But Gareth did not heed their taunts. For, indeed, he was a dreamer with a gift for seeing and interpreting the dreams of others.

And so it was that Terry Venables did favour Gareth and bestowed upon him the gift of a special waistcoat, woven from luxurious cloth of many colours. And, lo, the waistcoat was elegant, the cut was fine, the tasteful style was the ultimate in good design. And upon wearing the waistcoat of many colours was Gareth blessed with the most miraculous effect on his confidence on the pitch and his skill in defence. And thus did the waistcoat of many colours help Gareth prevent the opposition from scoring many goals. But so it was that the waistcoat of many colours did make Gareth's brothers yet more hateful and jealous still, for it did make him look even more posh. But Gareth did not heed their jealousy nor their hatefulness. And one night, the dreamer dreamed a most strange and marvellous dream whereupon he beheld eleven sheaves of corn.

Thus, upon awakening, Gareth put on his waistcoat of many colours and went to his brothers and said unto them: 'Lo, I pray you, heed the dream that I have dreamed. For I dreamed a dream that in the England football fields stood eleven sheaves of corn – one sheaf for each of us. And then did I behold that ten of the corn sheaves did bow their heads in obedience to a sheaf wearing a waistcoat of many colours and did listen intently to the sheaf's wise teachings and training methods, and then arrange themselves in a 3–5–2 formation.'

But the brothers were displeased with the dream that Gareth had dreamed, for to them it did seem as if the dream was indeed yet more proof that their brother was posher than them. Plus, whoever heard of a formation with only three at the back? And so, it came to pass that the brothers began to plot and scheme. And, one day after Gareth did miss an important penalty, the brothers made to capture him and strip him of his waistcoat of many colours, and thus they did sell Gareth to some passing slavers from Aston Villa for a small transfer fee.

And the brothers did take Gareth's waistcoat of many colours and cover it in the blood of a goat, as if it were his own, and said unto all who dwelt in Wembley: 'This is the waistcoat of many colours that we have found. Know now whether it is the amazing technicolour waistcoat of Gareth and that he has been rent in pieces by a savage, wild beast and met with a most sad and grisly end.' And they showed the sleeveless garment to Terry Venables, and he was so saddened that he stood down as manager of England's football fields (even though the FA had technically already replaced him with Glenn Hoddle).

And so, Gareth did toil in slavery for many years in the far-away land of Birmingham, where he was forced to make adverts for Pizza Hut and wear a bag upon his head. But still he did continue to follow his dreams. And his talent for interpreting the dreams of others (combined with his skill in defence and a generally likeable personality) made him renowned among the people of Aston Villa.

And thus it was that in the neighbouring land, the Pharaoh of Middlesbrough, Steve McClaren, was much troubled by dreams he had dreamed. Yet no one in this land could interpret the dreams that he had dreamed. And so, the Pharaoh's manservant did speak unto his master about a slave of great renown who dwelt among the people of Aston Villa and who, it was said, could understand the dreams of any man. And it came to pass that Gareth was brought before the Pharaoh, who said unto him: 'Hear this, Gareth. For this is the dream that I have dreamed. In a field, I beheld eleven well-fed cattle and eleven lean and ill-favoured cattle. And, lo, did the eleven lean-fleshed cattle beat the eleven well-fed cattle in a match of balls lasting but ninety minutes.'

And thus Gareth spake unto the Pharaoh with the clarity of Denis Norden, saying: 'The dream that thou hast dreamed is thus. The lean-fleshed cattle are the people of Middlesbrough. Though they will suffer much hardship and famine, they will defeat Bolton Wanderers 2–1 and win the League Cup in the 2003–04 season cup final." And so impressed was the Pharaoh by Gareth's wisdom, that he did provide Gareth with a well-paid job. And thus did Gareth prosper for many years, first as player for Middlesbrough, then as player-manager, then as manager of the national Under-21 squad. Visitors would travel from far and wide to seek Gareth's sage council and heed his wise words of wisdom about the dreams they had dreamed.

And so it came to pass that, one day, among the visitors to his house were faces that Gareth did recognise. For there came among them ten men whom he had once called brothers. For they had come to ask for the great dreamer's sage advice, yet when they stood before him still they did not recognise their brother, for he was older and wiser and more prosperous and had grown a well-groomed beard. And so did they speak unto Gareth of how the once-great land of Wembley had suffered from many years of famine and misfortune and pleaded with him to help them make England's barren football fields fruitful once more.

And lo did Gareth behold his brothers bowing their heads in obedience and listening intently to his wise teachings and training methods, just as in the dream he had dreamed. And Gareth did pity their wretchedness and thus did he reveal his true identity unto them, and they did know him by the poshness of his voice and did call him 'Nord'. And so, with tears of joy, they did welcome Gareth back to Wembley and make him the manager of all the football fields in England. And, filled with remorse and regret for their wrongdoings, the brothers returned unto him the waistcoat of many colours (having washed off the goat's blood with Vanish). And Gareth was most pleased. For how he loved his waistcoat of many colours. Such a dazzling coat of many colours. It was red and yellow and green and brown and scarlet and black and ochre and peach and ruby and olive and violet and fawn and lilac and gold and chocolate and mauve and cream and crimson and silver and rose and azure and lemon and russet and grey and purple and white and pink and orange and blue.

The En

Pizza Hunt

Gareth has missed another penalty and now he's working for a famous pizza restaurant chain again, just like he did in 1996, this time as a chef.

But – oh no! – he's lost the sizzling-hot pizza he has just baked.

Help Gareth find his way through the clouds of pizza steam so that he can serve his delicious pizza to Chris Waddle and Stuart Pearce.

GARETH IS THE BOSS-WORD

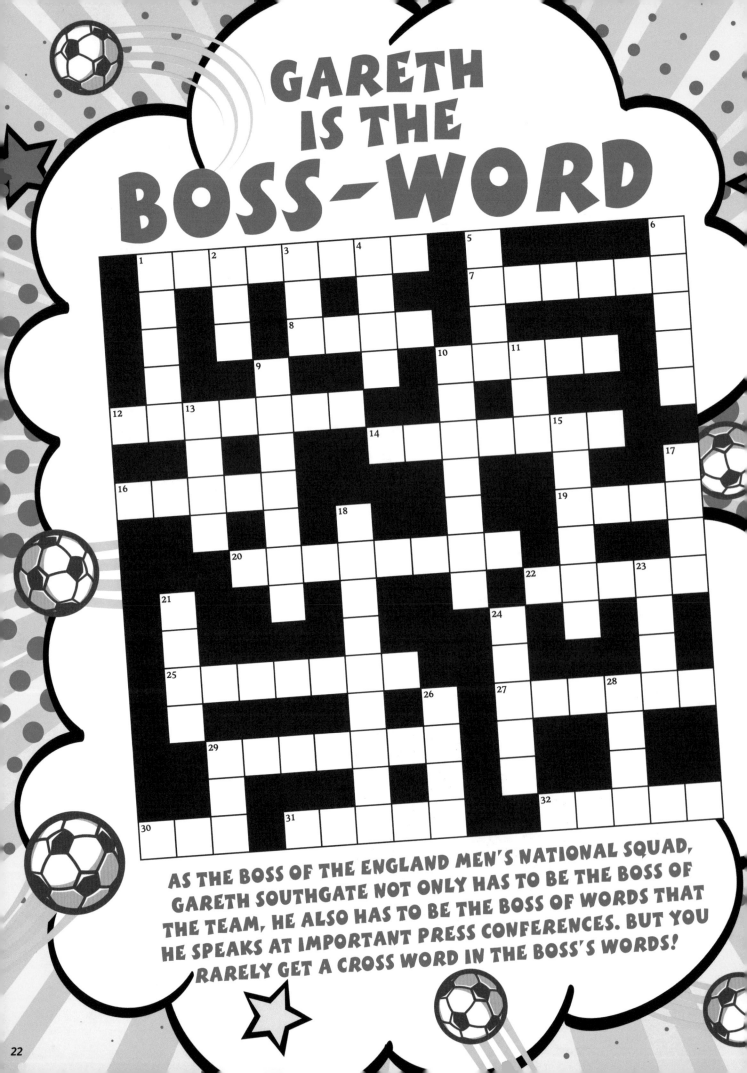

AS THE BOSS OF THE ENGLAND MEN'S NATIONAL SQUAD, GARETH SOUTHGATE NOT ONLY HAS TO BE THE BOSS OF THE TEAM, HE ALSO HAS TO BE THE BOSS OF WORDS THAT HE SPEAKS AT IMPORTANT PRESS CONFERENCES. BUT YOU RARELY GET A CROSS WORD IN THE BOSS'S WORDS!

ACROSS

1 Place on the pitch and in the team (8)
7 If 'Sir' Gareth, his honorary title is? (6)
8 Gareth is part of the human ____ (4)
10 What Gareth's choice of keeper, Pickford, needs to do to the ball (5)
12 Team leader, Kane (7)
14 Gareth's choice of inflatable fun (7)
16 The main artery in the heart that blood pumps through when England score six goals (5)
19 Nickname for team Gareth was player-manager of (4)
20 El Tel surname (8)
22 Gareth's facial hair (5)
25 What he missed in '96 (7)
27 Eden _____ scorer of second Belgium goal in Russia 2018 runners-up match (6)
29 Gareth's place of birth (7)
30 Gareth's birth___ on 3rd September (3)
31 (and 32 across) Team Gareth led to the 2000 FA Cup final (5, 5)
32 See 31 across

DOWN

1 Hut that Gareth advertised with Waddle and Pearce (5)
2 England super ___ Rashford (3)
3 A hill or rocky peak (3)
4 Number of times England won world cup (4)
5 World cup quarters foes' favourite shop (4)
6 What Gareth prefers to do at the dug-out (5)
9 Gareth's official position (7)
10 See 15 down
11 Number of children Gareth has (3)
13 Not mixed – joy that Gareth's England brings us (4)
15 (and 10 down) Joke poultry used in training (6, 7)
17 Gareth's old nickname (4)
18 Sleeveless upper body garment worn by Gareth (9)
21 What Gareth has brought the nation of supporters (4)
23 The three lions shout (4)
24 England's _____ and pains after training (5)
26 ____ Hazard scorer of second Belgium goal in Russia 2018 runners-up match (4)
28 Biblical Harry's brother (4)
29 Wembley ___ (3)

GARETH'S WORLD OF CUPS

IKEA plastic cup

Stein

Espresso cup

Bone china cup and saucer

Chimarrao cup

Breakfast cup (bowl)

GARETH HAS COLLECTED MANY CUPS FROM AROUND THE WORLD AS SOUVENIRS – HIS WORLD CUPS. BUT HE HAS BEEN CLEANING HIS WORLD CUP SHELVES AND THEY'VE ALL GOT JUMBLED UP. NOW HE CAN'T REMEMBER WHICH WORLD CUP COMES FROM WHICH COUNTRY! PLAY GARETH'S 'WORLD OF CUPS' WORLD CUP GAME AND MATCH EACH OF THE WORLD CUPS ON GARETH'S SHELVES WITH THEIR NATIONAL FLAG.

Germany

England

France

SOUTHGATE'S
NATIONAL TREASURES

Treasury XI

DEFENCE

MANAGER

GARETH **SOUTHGATE**
MANAGER

SPEED	78
CHARISMA	88
POWER	66
HUGS	95

NT INDEX **90**

FOOTBALL SKILLZ **100**

GOALKEEPER

STEPHEN **FRY**
GOALKEEPER

SPEED	16
CHARISMA	72
POWER	98
HUGS	89

NT INDEX **85**

FOOTBALL SKILLZ **4**

LEFT BACK

MARY **BERRY**
LEFT BACK

SPEED	84
CHARISMA	14
POWER	17
HUGS	94

NT INDEX **88**

FOOTBALL SKILLZ **50**

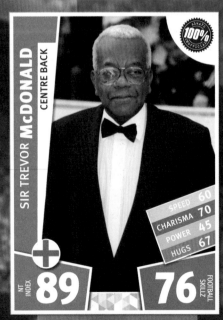

SIR TREVOR **McDONALD**
CENTRE BACK

SPEED	60
CHARISMA	70
POWER	45
HUGS	67

NT INDEX **89**

FOOTBALL SKILLZ **76**

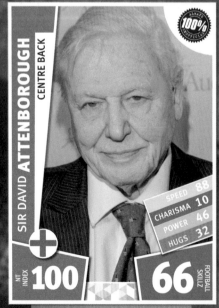

SIR DAVID **ATTENBOROUGH**
CENTRE BACK

SPEED	88
CHARISMA	10
POWER	46
HUGS	32

NT INDEX **100**

FOOTBALL SKILLZ **66**

DELIA **SMITH**
RIGHT BACK

SPEED	56
CHARISMA	08
POWER	78
HUGS	12

NT INDEX **79**

FOOTBALL SKILLZ **89**

11 ????? 10 ????? 9 ?????

6 ????? 7 ????? 8 ?????

4 Berry 2 McDonald 3 Attenbourough 5 Smith

1 Fry

LEFT MID

CENTRE MID

RIGHT MID

?

?

?

?

?

?

LEFT WING

CENTRE FORWARD

RIGHT WING

CUT-OUT-AND-KEEP
DANCING GARETH
WAISTCOAT DOLL

GARETH IS A MOVER AND SHAKER IN THE WORLD OF FOOTBALL MANAGEMENT. BUT DID YOU KNOW HE CAN ALSO SHAKE HIS BOOTY ON THE DANCE FLOOR?

SIMPLY CUT OUT GARETH'S HEAD, LIMBS AND TORSO FROM THIS PAGE, PIN THEM TOGETHER

AND WATCH HIM BOOGIE!

PSYCHIC
SOUTHGATE'S
HOROSCOPES

As the brightest star in the footballing firmament, Gareth has had to keep his gaze fixed firmly on the England men's team's future. But what if he could forecast your future, too? Using only the latest techniques and futuristic terminology, we predict what Gareth would predict, if he were to predict your future.

ARIES

March 21 – April 19

Strong willed, ambitious and passionate

A massive bulbous lunar event in late July, just as Aquarius ascends the star space. Jupiter resists an emotional Scorpio from August backwards through August, making you ever more psychic.
Only blue on June 11th.

FAMOUS FOOTBALL ARIANS
Ronaldinho

TAURUS

April 20 – May 20

Generous, stubborn and selfish

In the summer month of winter, Mars is retrospect in early Aquarius, and then Apricorns, and then the other ones. Realign and reproduce great magnetic energy up and at 'em.

FAMOUS FOOTBALL TAUREANS
David Beckham

GEMINI

May 21 – June 20

Energetic, superficial and impulsive

The Venus principle isn't retrograde from Octoberfest through the first minute to two and a half of November, ending in Libra, impacts your tooth more.
Love will resolve unnecessarily.

FAMOUS FOOTBALL GEMINITES
George Best

CANCER

June 21 – July 22

Loyal, moody, self-pitying

Your Mars bar is retractable from its upgrade late June through later in later June. Life won't always work, love. Get a grip. Mars bar retro in Aquarius and Copernicus encourages you to make your social life and work more sturdy.

FAMOUS FOOTBALL CANCERIAN
Lionel Messi

LEO

July 23 – August 22

Ambitious, domineering, melodramatic

Your Noodle Node is now in Leo now. Events up in your life spin round and backbite in karmic reverse. A partial solar eclipse in August could affect your bowels. Prepare the prunes!

FAMOUS FOOTBALL LEONS
Harry Kane

VIRGO

August 23 – September 22

Helpful, fussy, inflexible

The sun conjoins your modern metal-loving planet, Bluto, which is reasonable. All earth signs of Capricorn are gone, my dear, leaving only despair and sorrow. The sun always shines on TV.

FAMOUS FOOTBALL VIRGINS
Gareth Southgate

LIBRA

September 23 – October 22

Peaceful, superficial, indecisive

Just after Apollo Creed turns lucid in November, your planet Mercury conjoins masterful Jupiter for five minutes flat. Your high life needs more inflation at this juncture. Behave yourself.

FAMOUS FOOTBALL LIBRANS
Alexandra Scott

SCORPIO

October 23 – November 21

Passionate, obsessive, suspicious

Your planet is making a slow transition back and forth and back and forth through Uranus from time to time and time to time. You will resonate well in Glasgow.

FAMOUS FOOTBALL SCORPIONS
Diego Maradona

SAGITTARIUS

November 22 – December 21

Selfless, independent, unemotional

Weak solar seeds prevent Mars from fluctuating and undulating during early Thursday. Remove the lunar entry to facilitate a finer illusion of raucous with Saturn. Try another year next year.

FAMOUS FOOTBALL SAGITTARIANS
Kylian Mbappé

CAPRICORN

December 22 – January 19

Patient, dictatorial, distrusting

When the sun enters Leo, Venus is already there hiding. Hello, there! In October, Venus goes direct to Libra (do not pass go) in November – not too good for your health!

FAMOUS FOOTBALL CAPRICOTS
Eden Hazard

AQUARIUS

January 20 – February 18

Witty, unemotional, sarcastic

The all-splicing Mars-Neptune conglomerate in Gemini may tug at your coat tails, but when Sportacus gets going, the Sun is joined by Crockett and Tubbs. Jupiter and Mercury prizes await!

FAMOUS FOOTBALL AQUARIUMS
Cristiano Ronaldo

PISCES

February 19 – March 20

Compassionate, indecisive, self-pitying

Saturn is upper retrograde in Capricorn One from April/June/July until early September/October/November. Late August and early September will be much too electric times for you. .

FAMOUS FOOTBALL PESCETARIANS
Kenny Dalglish

SOUTHGATE'S STYLISH DUG-OUT FASHION DOs AND DON'TS

Gareth understands that to be a successful football manager, you need to cut a dashing figure on the touchline. We all know about Gareth's famous waistcoat, but here are some other fashion tips from the best-dressed football managers around.

JOACHIM LÖW
When the elements are against you on the touchline, dress for the weather, but don't lose your integrity.

DO . . . wear high-fashion mohair or cashmere scarves and sleek, stylish waterproofs for wet weather – Karl Lagerfeld or Hugo Boss, for example.

DON'T . . . bother with the sheepskin coat. It's a cliché and just doesn't cut it on the modern pitch-side.

JOSÉ MOURINHO
Dress in the classics, but make them your own

DO . . . add your own personal twists, such as a rakishly loosened tie

DON'T . . . be a slave to convention. There's such a thing as too classic

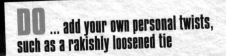

PEP GUARDIOLA
A stylish woolen can enhance even the most straightforward outfit

DO ... wear a slim-fit lambswool V-neck over a shirt and tie.

DON'T ... choose the wrong lambswool sweater – or the wrong tie.

MAURICIO POCHETTINO
If you have to wear a track suit pitch-side, always show discretion.

DO ... choose a tracksuit that complements your body shape and flatters your natural physique.

DON'T ... be Roy Hodgson.

33

THE PENALTIES OF LOVE

It's the 1980s and dishy Gareth is at a crossroads – should he continue as a world-famous snogging model or follow his dream of soccer stardom?

A GARETH LOVE STORY

STARRING
the young
TONY HADLEY
as the young
GARETH SOUTHGATE

Gareth was in the park with snogging model partner and friend, Roxy...

I'VE BEEN APPROACHED BY CRYSTAL PALACE SOCCER SIDE. THEY WANT ME TO PLAY FOR THEM AND EVENTUALLY BECOME THEIR CAPTAIN!

IS THAT WHY YOU'RE LOOKING AT YOUR HANDS?

YES. IT HELPS ME MAKE DECISIONS. LOOKING AT THE SKY ALSO HELPS, SOMETIMES. WHAT SHOULD I DO ROXY? SNOGGING OR SOCCER?

WELL, YOU'RE SO GOOD AT BOTH – SNOGGING ME AND SOCCER. I'M ONLY GOOD AT SNOGGING. WHAT ELSE COULD I DO?

MAYBE SOMETHING WITH YOUR HANDS? THEY'RE SO VERSATILE AND ATHLETIC. ANYWAY, LET'S PRACTISE FOR OUR PHOTO SHOOT.

Later, near some shrubs...

ALSO, HOW WOULD I TELL MONA, OUR MEAN-SPIRITED BOSS, THAT I MIGHT QUIT? DECISIONS...

I KNEW YOU WERE THINKING ABOUT DECISIONS 'COS YOU WERE LOOKING AT THE SKY. SHALL WE DO SOME RUNNING?

I DAREN'T TELL HIM I'M IN LOVE WITH HIM. IT'LL MAKE IT WORSE.

WEEEEEEEEEEEEEEEEE!! I LOVE RUNNING!

WE'RE RUNNING SO FAST! JUST LIKE GREYHOUNDS!

When they arrived at the photo shoot, mean Mona was waiting for them. And she wasn't happy...

YOU'RE LATE.

SORRY, MONA. WE WERE TALKING ABOUT DECISIONS AND LOST TRACK OF TIME.

Mona held on to the door frame and looked to her right-hand side, angrily...

AS LONG AS YOU'RE NOT HIDING ANY RUDDY SECRETS FROM ME.

OF COURSE NOT! GARETH DOESN'T EVEN LIKE SOCCER AND I DON'T EVEN SECRETLY LOVE HIM. SO...

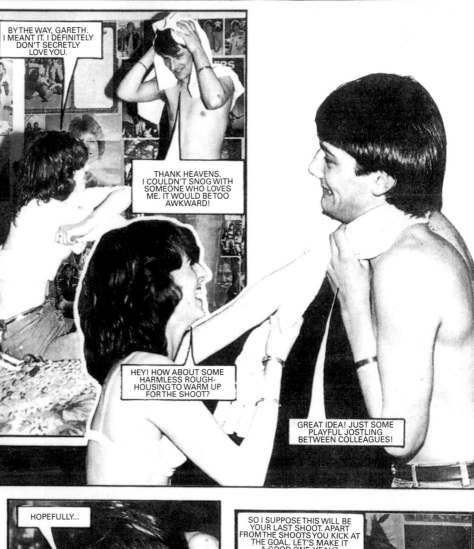

BY THE WAY, GARETH. I MEANT IT. I DEFINITELY DON'T SECRETLY LOVE YOU.

THANK HEAVENS. I COULDN'T SNOG WITH SOMEONE WHO LOVES ME. IT WOULD BE TOO AWKWARD!

HEY! HOW ABOUT SOME HARMLESS ROUGH-HOUSING TO WARM UP FOR THE SHOOT?

GREAT IDEA! JUST SOME PLAYFUL JOSTLING BETWEEN COLLEAGUES!

C'MON, GARETH, LET'S GET READY FOR OUR 1980s LIP GLOSS SNOGGING PHOTO SHOOT.

ROGER THAT.

BTW, I'VE DECIDED MY DECISION. I'M GONNA BE A SOCCER PLAYER AND LEAVE SNOG-MODELLING FOREVER.

I'LL BE SAD TO SEE YOU GO. BUT MAYBE YOU'LL MANAGE THE ENGLAND SOCCER TEAM ONE DAY!

HOPEFULLY...

YES.

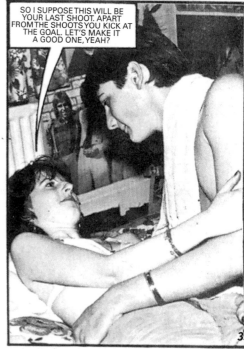

SO I SUPPOSE THIS WILL BE YOUR LAST SHOOT. APART FROM THE SHOOTS YOU KICK AT THE GOAL. LET'S MAKE IT A GOOD ONE, YEAH?

35

I SECRETLY LOVE GARETH. BUT, LIKE THE FAMOUS 1980s STING SONG SAYS, 'IF YOU LOVE SOMEONE, LET THEM GO'. SO, BECAUSE I SECRETLY LOVE YOU, GARETH, I'M GOING TO LET YOU GO. EVEN THOUGH YOU DON'T KNOW I LOVE YOU.

OI! YOU TWO DUH-BRAINS!

STOP SNOGGING FOR PRACTICE AND SNOG FOR THE CAMERA INSTEAD!

YEAH! THAT'S IT! SNOG HIM REAL GOOD! PHWOAR! REALLY RANDY! THAT'S FLIPPIN' LOVELY! SNOG HIM LIKE YOU MEAN IT!

BUT I DO REALLY MEAN IT!!

A couple of days later, Mona was stipulating the schedule for the week's forthcoming snog-modelling shoot agenda...

...SO, WE ARRIVE IN BOSTON AT 08.00HRS EASTERN STANDARD TIME. THERE'LL BE A LIMO TO TAKE YOU, ME AND GARETH TO THE SHOOT. WHERE IS GARETH, BY THE WAY?

YEAH... ABOUT THAT. GARETH'S GIVEN UP SNOG-MODELLING. AND I'M GOING SOLO.

GOING SOLO? DON'T BE A FLIPPIN' IDIOT! THERE'S NO SUCH THING AS A 'SOLO' SNOG MODELLER! STUPID COW! YOU AND THAT STUPID HUNKY SOCCER BALL PLAYER HAVE RUINED EVERYTHING! RIGHT...

...NOW YOU'RE JUST GONNA HAVE TO SNOG THIS SLIGHTLY SCARY 1980s CLOTH CLOWN THAT I AM HOLDING HERE IN MY HAND INSTEAD! HE'S YOUR NEW SNOGGING PARTNER!

MR BANJO? NO! I CAN'T SNOG HIM!!

LOOK, YOU RUDDY SLAG! THESE PHOTOS ARE MY LIVELIHOOD. AND YOURS, TOO. YOU NEED THE DOSH! AND YOU NEED ME. I MADE YOU. AND YOU'RE ONLY GOOD FOR ONE THING: SNOGGING!

YOU'RE WRONG! LOOK AT THESE HANDS! I CAN BE WHATEVER I WANT! AN OLYMPIC HURDLER, FOR EXAMPLE!

Roxy showed Mona her versatile, athletic hands.

PAH! GUNNELL SCHMUNNELL! SOUTHGATE SCHMOUTHGATE!! I DON'T NEED EITHER OF YOU OR YOUR SPORTING AMBITIONS. ME AND MR BANJO HERE ARE GOING TO BE BIGGER THAN THE BOTH OF YOU! WE'LL GET A BLACK BOARD, SOME CHALK AND A CUTE LITTLE GIRL AND TAKE A PHOTO THAT BECOMES FAMOUS FOR ALL TIME!!

DON'T BE A DAFTY! YOU WOULDN'T SURVIVE THREE MINUTES ON THE MEAN STREETS OF SAXMUNDHAM WITHOUT ME, ROXY!

I SECRETLY LOVED GARETH, AND HE INSPIRED ME TO FOLLOW MY DREAMS. AND DON'T CALL ME ROXY! MY REAL NAME'S SALLY. SALLY GUNNELL.

And that's how the BBC test card was invented, folks!

THE END

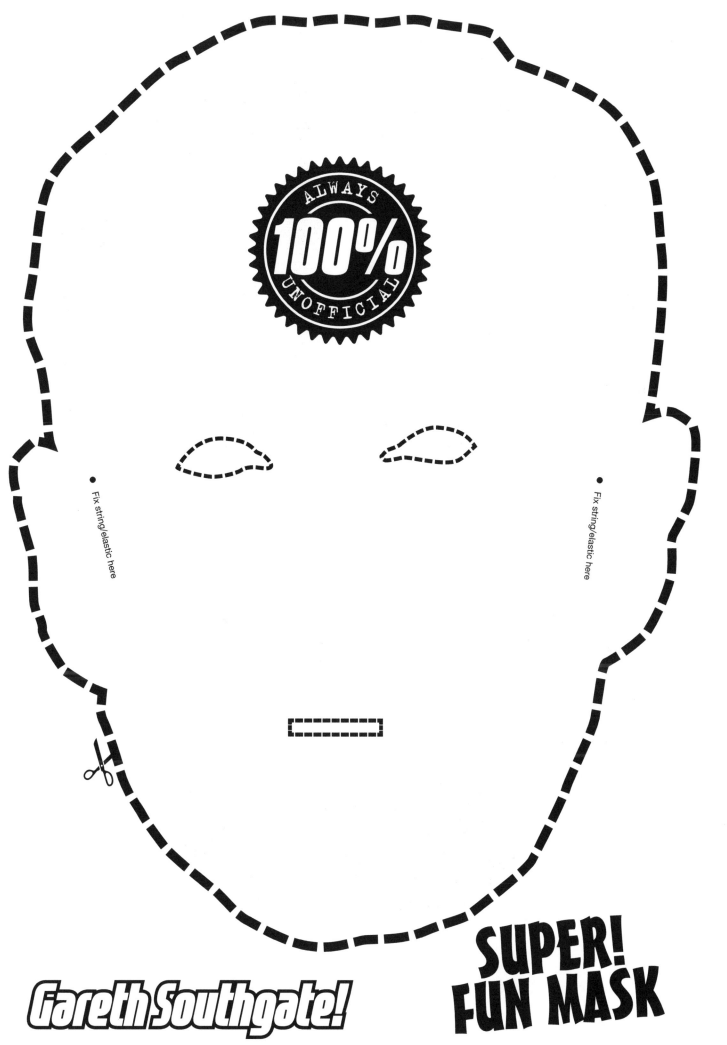

ALWAYS 100% UNOFFICIAL

Fix string/elastic here

Fix string/elastic here

Gareth Southgate!

SUPER!
FUN MASK

Gareth Southgate!

SUPER!
FUN MASK

THE WORLD'S No.1 SEXIEST MAN(AGER)

SAINT
GARETH

GARETH SOUTHGATE

...UP 2022...ALIGHT HERE FOR EURO 2020 AND QATAR WORLD CUP 2022...ALIGHT HE

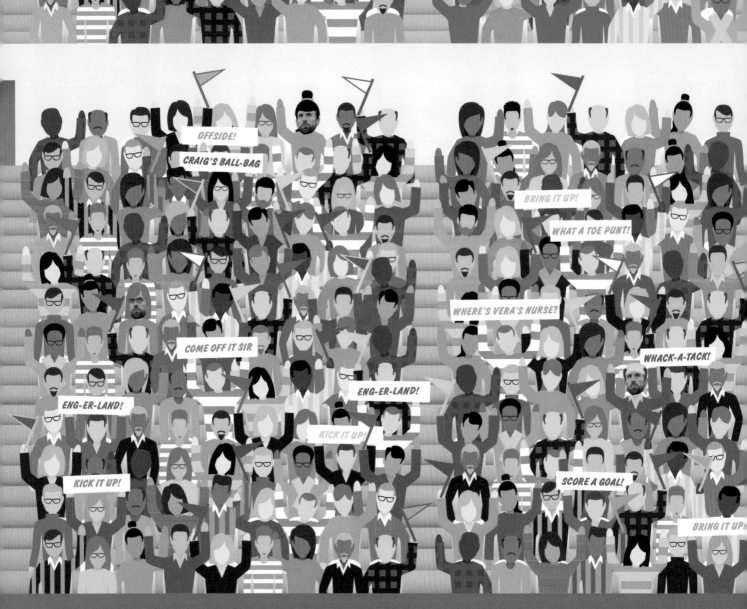

THE GREAT GARETH HUNT GAME

THERE'S AN ENTIRE TEAM OF GARETHS HIDDEN IN THIS FOOTBALL CROWD. SEE IF YOU CAN HUNT DOWN ALL ELEVEN!

PROFESSOR SOUTHGATENSTEIN'S LAB

Imagine you're Professor Southgatenstein – the world's greatest mad scientist football manager. Using safety scissors you must create the ultimate footballer by cutting out the best bits of players past and present and 'splicing' them together using sticky tape – or glitter glue, for extra sparkle!

Harry Maguire's monolithic slabhead

Kevin Keegan's curly soccerlocks

David Seaman's Super Mario tache

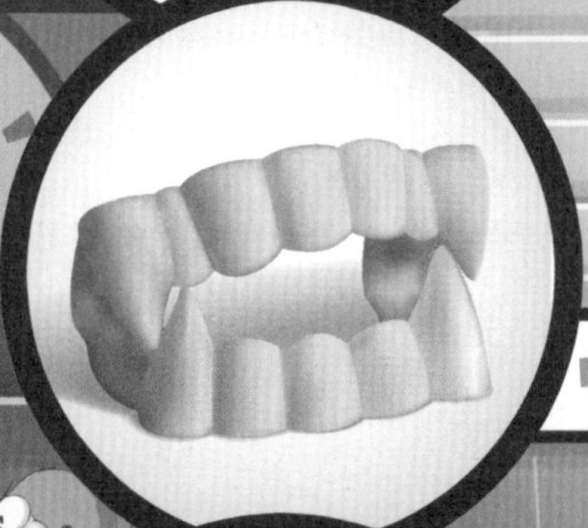

Luis Suarez's man-eating gnashers

Jimmy Hill's whopping great chin

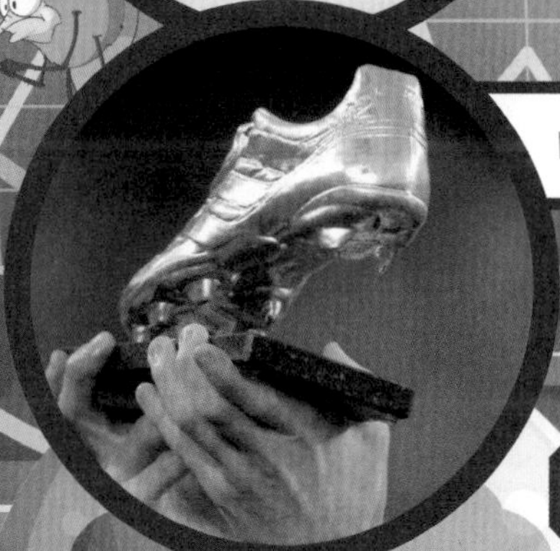

Lionel Messi's golden boots

David Beckham's golden balls

Gordon Banks's miraculous right hand

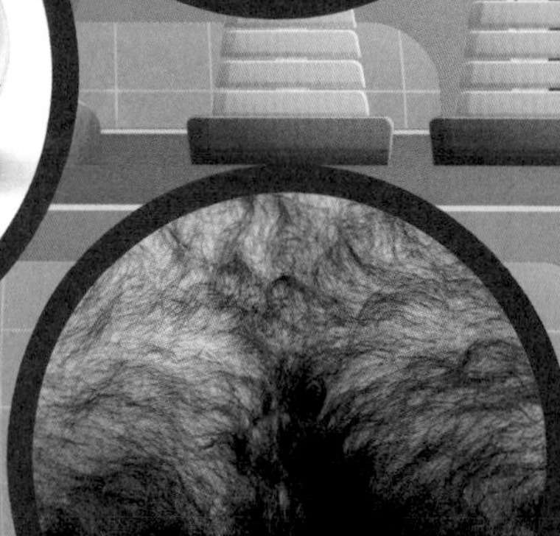

Maradona's even more miraculous left hand

Ryan Giggs's magnificent chest rug

47

SOUTHGATE'S GATES OF ENGLAND

GARETH SOUTHGATE ISN'T THE ONLY GREAT 'GATE IN THE COUNTRY. HERE IS A CELEBRATION OF SOME OF ENGLAND'S GREATEST GATES OF ALL TIME.

Classic rustic English gate (wood and iron), set in a drystone wall in the village of Bibury, Gloucestershire, approximately 76 miles (via the A41) from where Gareth was born in Watford.

Railway ticket barrier gates (stainless steel and rubber compound), with contactless pad and hard ticket entry slot in Kings Cross train station, where Gareth would arrive if he took a train to London from his current home in Harrogate, North Yorkshire.

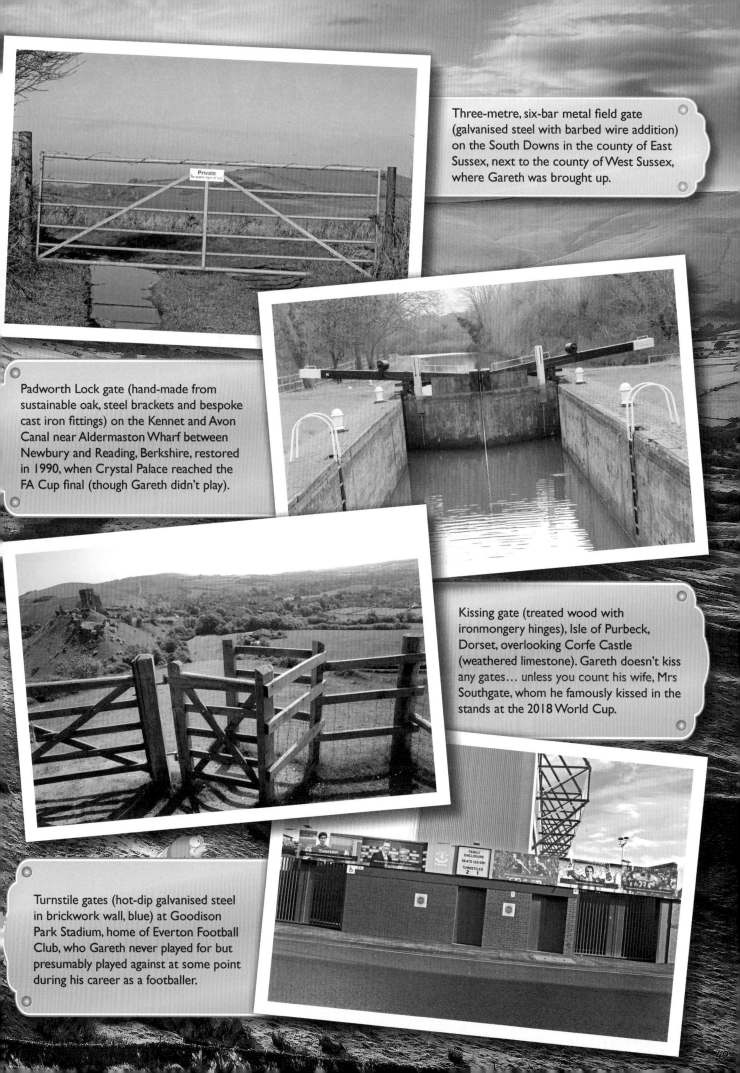

Three-metre, six-bar metal field gate (galvanised steel with barbed wire addition) on the South Downs in the county of East Sussex, next to the county of West Sussex, where Gareth was brought up.

Private
No public right of way

Padworth Lock gate (hand-made from sustainable oak, steel brackets and bespoke cast iron fittings) on the Kennet and Avon Canal near Aldermaston Wharf between Newbury and Reading, Berkshire, restored in 1990, when Crystal Palace reached the FA Cup final (though Gareth didn't play).

Kissing gate (treated wood with ironmongery hinges), Isle of Purbeck, Dorset, overlooking Corfe Castle (weathered limestone). Gareth doesn't kiss any gates… unless you count his wife, Mrs Southgate, whom he famously kissed in the stands at the 2018 World Cup.

Turnstile gates (hot-dip galvanised steel in brickwork wall, blue) at Goodison Park Stadium, home of Everton Football Club, who Gareth never played for but presumably played against at some point during his career as a footballer.

FAMILY ENCLOSURE SEATS 172-251 TURNSTILES 2 1

SOUTHGATE'S
SWEET FA
PARTY TREATS

Pitch Shaped Team-Talk Toast

Ingredients: Toast, butter/margarine.

Simply scrape the shape of a football pitch onto the toast with a knife then spread the toast with butter or margarine. Now you're ready to kick off this party and be the 'toast' of the FA.

Pepperoni Penalty Pizza

Ingredients: Pizza, pepperoni slices, anchovies

Make 'panel' shapes on the pizza with the anchovies then fill the 'panels' with pepperoni slices. **Warning:** anchovies are disgusting so you might want to use a felt tip pen to draw the panels on the pizza instead. 'Spot the ball? What ball? It's already been eaten, ref.'

Every once in a while Gareth likes to throw a little party to thank and reward his players and backroom staff for all their hard work. Here are some of the delicious delicacies Gareth might like to serve his footballing friends.
Perhaps you can try them at home.

Chocolate Waffle Wall

Ingredients: Waffles, liquid chocolate.

Arrange the waffles in a defensive wall and then bind them together with the liquid chocolate. That's one wall you wouldn't mind getting stuck into!

World Cup-Cakes

Ingredients: Fairy cakes, green icing, small fondant footballs

Ice the fairy cakes with the green icing to suggest a football pitch then place the fondant football on top. These treats won't make it to extra time, that's for sure!

SOUTHGATE'S
NATIONAL TREASURES

Treasury XI

MIDFIELD

MANAGER

GARETH **SOUTHGATE**
MANAGER

SPEED	78
CHARISMA	88
POWER	66
HUGS	95

NT INDEX **90**

FOOTBALL SKILLZ **100**

GOALKEEPER

STEPHEN **FRY**
GOALKEEPER

SPEED	16
CHARISMA	72
POWER	98
HUGS	89

NT INDEX **85**

FOOTBALL SKILLZ **4**

LEFT BACK

MARY **BERRY**
LEFT BACK

SPEED	84
CHARISMA	14
POWER	17
HUGS	94

NT INDEX **88**

FOOTBALL SKILLZ **50**

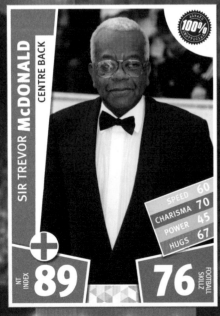

SIR TREVOR **McDONALD**
CENTRE BACK

SPEED	60
CHARISMA	70
POWER	45
HUGS	67

NT INDEX **89**

FOOTBALL SKILLZ **76**

CENTRE BACK

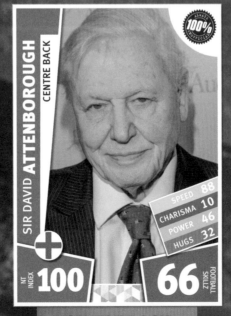

SIR DAVID **ATTENBOROUGH**
CENTRE BACK

SPEED	88
CHARISMA	10
POWER	46
HUGS	32

NT INDEX **100**

FOOTBALL SKILLZ **66**

CENTRE BACK

DELIA **SMITH**
RIGHT BACK

SPEED	56
CHARISMA	08
POWER	78
HUGS	12

NT INDEX **79**

FOOTBALL SKILLZ **89**

RIGHT BACK

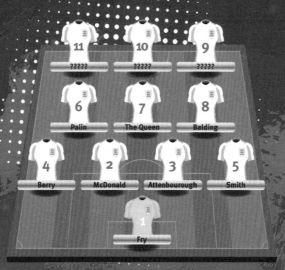

11 ?????	
10 ?????	
9 ?????	
6 Palin	
7 The Queen	
8 Balding	
4 Berry	
2 McDonald	
3 Attenbourough	
5 Smith	
1 Fry	

LEFT MID

MICHAEL **PALIN**
LEFT MID

100%

SPEED	16
CHARISMA	91
POWER	10
HUGS	92

NT INDEX **91**

70 FOOTBALL SKILLZ

CENTRE MID

THE **QUEEN** (CAPTAIN)
CENTRE MID

100%

SPEED	88
CHARISMA	52
POWER	100
HUGS	98

NT INDEX **87**

98 FOOTBALL SKILLZ

RIGHT MID

CLARE **BALDING**
RIGHT MID

100%

SPEED	68
CHARISMA	70
POWER	44
HUGS	17

NT INDEX **87**

33 FOOTBALL SKILLZ

?

?

?

LEFT WING

CENTRE FORWARD

RIGHT WING

SOUTHGATE'S CELEBRITY BEAR-GROOMING TIPS

Gareth is a modern man – he isn't ashamed to take care of his appearance. But, as England manager, he needs to be able to leap into action at a moment's notice. Here's some of the advice Gareth might offer other hirsute heroes for quickly taming that facial hair.

HAGRID

JEREMY CORBYN

DON'T BUG ME

Consider using a citronella oil-based balm on your beard, as it can also act as an insect repellent for when the pitch is invaded by swarms of mosquitos, midges or Death Eaters during early group matches.

OIL'S WELL

Take five minutes to apply beard oil every evening. That way you won't ever need to oil your beard during the day when you might have an important match or training session or Labour Party conference.

CONCHITA WURST

BRUSH IT OFF

Keep a beard brush and moustache comb with you at all times. A small grooming set can be easily tucked into a waistcoat pocket or a handbag.

ZZ TOP

DON'T BE A FLAKE

Use beard shampoos and conditioners with natural ingredients to avoid skin irritation and flakiness. No player is going to take you seriously with beardruff all over your waistcoat! Remember – every girl's crazy 'bout a sharp-dressed man!

B. A. BARACAS

CUT IT OUT

Between trips to the barbers, use a pair of beard scissors to keep your facial hair tidy so you never lose that nonchalant 'just got to the semis' look. While you're at it, why not trim your Mohican, fool?

SANTA CLAUS

BUTTER UP

Apply a beard butter or wax to keep those bristles in line. The last thing you want is an unruly facial hair breaking formation when attending a post-match press conference or performing a Christmas miracle.

GARETH BY NUMBERS

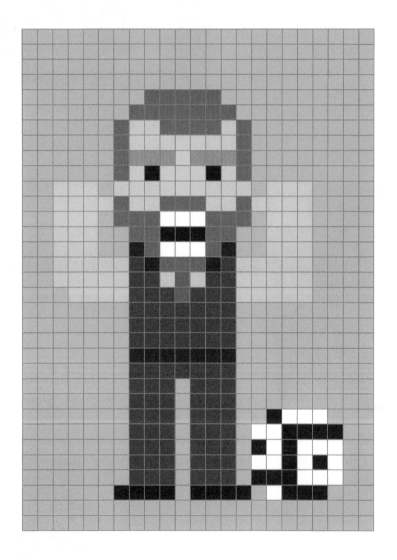

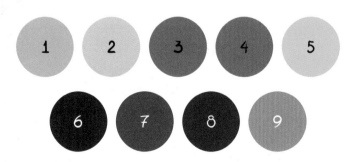

1	1	1	1	1	1	1	1	1	1	1	1	1	1	1	1	1	1	1	1	1	1	1	1	1	1	1	1
1	1	1	1	1	1	1	1	1	1	1	1	1	1	1	1	1	1	1	1	1	1	1	1	1	1	1	1
1	1	1	1	1	1	1	1	1	1	1	1	1	1	1	1	1	1	1	1	1	1	1	1	1	1	1	1
1	1	1	1	1	1	1	1	1	1	1	1	1	1	1	1	1	1	1	1	1	1	1	1	1	1	1	1
1	1	1	1	1	1	1	1	4	4	4	4	4	1	1	1	1	1	1	1	1	1	1	1	1	1	1	1
1	1	1	1	1	1	1	4	4	4	4	4	4	4	1	1	1	1	1	1	1	1	1	1	1	1	1	1
1	1	1	1	1	1	4	5	5	4	4	4	4	5	4	1	1	1	1	1	1	1	1	1	1	1	1	1
1	1	1	1	1	1	4	5	5	5	5	5	5	5	4	1	1	1	1	1	1	1	1	1	1	1	1	1
1	1	1	1	1	1	4	9	9	9	5	9	9	9	4	1	1	1	1	1	1	1	1	1	1	1	1	1
1	1	1	1	1	1	4	5	6	5	5	5	6	5	4	1	1	1	1	1	1	1	1	1	1	1	1	1
1	1	5	5	5	1	5	5	5	5	5	5	5	5	5	1	5	5	5	1	1	1	1	1	1	1	1	1
1	1	5	5	5	5	4	5	5	4	4	4	5	5	4	5	5	5	5	1	1	1	1	1	1	1	1	1
1	1	5	5	5	1	4	4	4			4	4	4	1	5	5	5	1	1	1	1	1	1	1	1	1	1
1	1	2	2	2	1	1	4	4	6	6	6	4	4	1	1	2	2	2	1	1	1	1	1	1	1	1	1
1	1	2	2	2	1	1	8	4			4	8	1	1	2	2	2	1	1	1	1	1	1	1	1	1	1
1	1	2	2	2	2	2	7	8	4	4	4	8	7	2	2	2	2	2	1	1	1	1	1	1	1	1	1
1	1	2	2	2	2	2	7	7	2	3	2	7	7	2	2	2	2	2	1	1	1	1	1	1	1	1	1
1	1	1	2	2	2	2	7	7	7	3	7	7	7	2	2	2	2	2	1	1	1	1	1	1	1	1	1
1	1	1	1	1	1	1	7	7	7	7	7	7	7	1	1	1	1	1	1	1	1	1	1	1	1	1	1
1	1	1	1	1	1	1	7	7	7	7	7	7	7	1	1	1	1	1	1	1	1	1	1	1	1	1	1
1	1	1	1	1	1	1	7	7	7	7	7	7	7	1	1	1	1	1	1	1	1	1	1	1	1	1	1
1	1	1	1	1	1	1	8	8	8	8	8	8	8	1	1	1	1	1	1	1	1	1	1	1	1	1	1
1	1	1	1	1	1	1	7	7	7	7	7	7	7	1	1	1	1	1	1	1	1	1	1	1	1	1	1
1	1	1	1	1	1	1	7	7	7	1	7	7	7	1	1	1	1	1	1	1	1	1	1	1	1	1	1
1	1	1	1	1	1	1	7	7	7	1	7	7	7	1	1	1	1	1	1	1	1	1	1	1	1	1	1
1	1	1	1	1	1	1	7	7	7	1	7	7	7	1	1	6									1	1	1
1	1	1	1	1	1	1	7	7	7	1	7	7	7	1								6	6	6	6	1	1
1	1	1	1	1	1	1	7	7	7	1	7	7	7	1	6									6		1	1
1	1	1	1	1	1	1	7	7	7	1	7	7	7	1			6						6		1	1	
1	1	1	1	1	1	1	7	7	7	1	7	7	7	1	6	6	6									1	1
1	1	1	1	1	1	6	6	6	6	1	6	6	6	6	1							6	6	6	1	1	1
1	1	1	1	1	1	1	1	1	1	1	1	1	1	1	1	1	1	1	1	1	1	1	1	1	1	1	1
1	1	1	1	1	1	1	1	1	1	1	1	1	1	1	1	1	1	1	1	1	1	1	1	1	1	1	1

GARETH'S 'A-MAZE-BALLS'
AMAZING FOOTBALL MAZE

England have finally made it to the World Cup final, but injuries have forced 'The Gaffer' to pull on his England jersey one more time. And now Pussy Riot have invaded the pitch! Although Gareth sympath with their concerns time is running out. Help Gareth weave his way through the human-rights protes to score the winning goal in the final minute and bring the cup home for England!

STOP!

EQUALITY!

EVERYBODY NEEDS HUGS

Nobody knows the importance of a good hug more than Gareth Southgate.

Whenever things go bad for his players, he's always there on the sidelines with his big, strong arms open wide, ready to hug away the sorrow and offer a tender, yet masculine shoulder to cry on. Sadly, Gareth can't be there for us all when we need a good hug. So, here is a selection of everyday cuddly buddies that anyone can snuggle up to, along with the huggability ratings that Gareth might have given them.

A PUPPY

Cuteness
8/10

Furry factor
9/10

Shoulder-to-cry-on-ability
2/10

Overall huggability
6.33/10

A GRAN

Cuteness
6/10

Furry factor
5/10

Shoulder-to-cry-on-ability
6/10

Overall huggability
5.66/10

A BABY PANDA

Cuteness
9/10

Furry factor
9/10

Shoulder-to-cry-on-ability
1/10

Overall huggability
6.33/10

A PRESIDENT OF THE UNITED STATES

Cuteness
6/10

Furry factor
7/10

Shoulder-to-cry-on-ability
0/10

Overall huggability
4.33/10

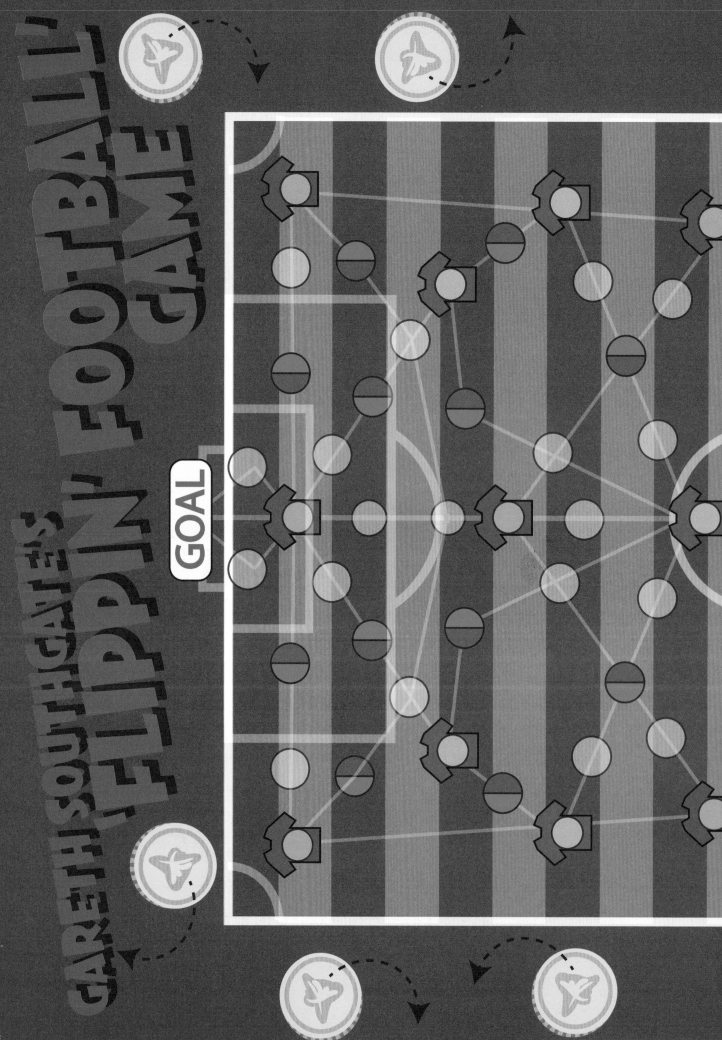

GARETH SOUTHGATE'S FLIPPIN' FOOTBALL GAME

GOAL

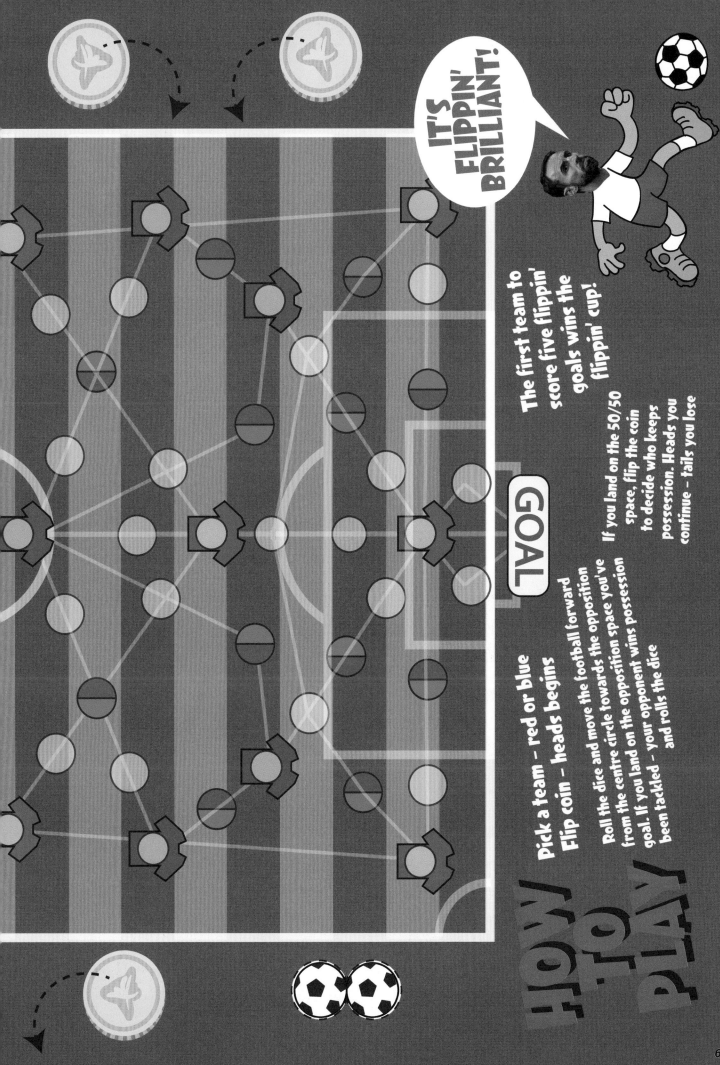

IT'S FLIPPIN' BRILLIANT!

GOAL

The first team to score five flippin' goals wins the flippin' cup!

If you land on the 50/50 space, flip the coin to decide who keeps possession. Heads you continue – tails you lose

Pick a team – red or blue
Flip coin – heads begins

Roll the dice and move the football forward from the centre circle towards the opposition goal. If you land on the opposition space you've been tackled – your opponent wins possession and rolls the dice

HOW TO PLAY

PIN THE WAISTCOAT
ON THE GARETH

AS ENGLAND'S MANAGER, GARETH ALWAYS LOOKS SMART, BUT IMAGINE HOW HE MIGHT HAVE LOOKED PITCH-SIDE IF HE'D CHOSEN A DIFFERENT WAISTCOAT.

CUT OUT THE WAISTCOATS OPPOSITE AND PIN THEM ONTO GARETH'S TORSO ABOVE.

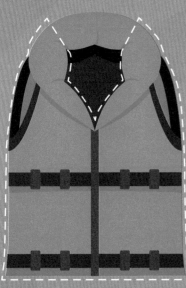

1 The Hasselhoff

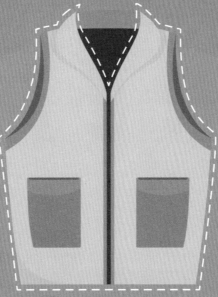

2 The Thrifty Pensioner

3 The Sculpted Scandinavian

4 The Health and Safety

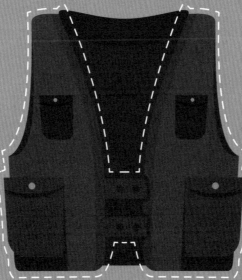

5 The Doomsday Survivalist

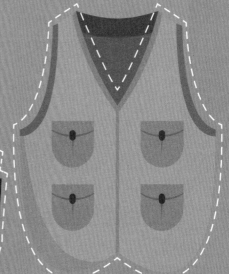

6 The Fisherman's Friend

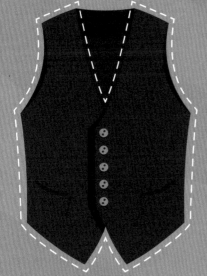

7 The Modern Manager

8 The Ribbed for Extra Pleasure

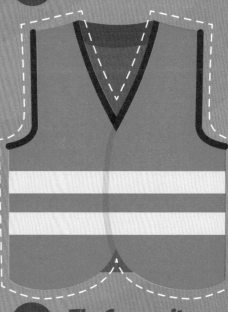

9 The Community Service

OTHER
GARETHS

**IF YOU ENJOY GARETH SOUTHGATE,
HERE'S A SELECTION OF OTHER GLORIOUS GARETHS FOR YOUR CONSIDERATION**

GATES

This crooning Gareth (34) is similar to Gareth Southgate, but with less 'south' (in his name). His winning smile will make your eyes pop (idol (runner-up (2002))) out of your head.

BALE

This 29-year-old Welsh footballing Gareth won't bail (Bale) on you if you're in a real (Madrid) pickle. Hey (hay), Bale! Better keep playing well or you'll never get into your namesake's England squad (if you weren't Welsh).

HUNT

New Avenger Hunt was an actor (in *The New Avengers*) and advert star, known for his smooth voice, good looks and bean-shaking abilities. Hunky Hunt was certainly an instant (coffee) hit with the ladies!

This choirmaster Gareth (43) is never (M)alone – he always has a big group of nurses and military wives (or similar) nearby. Not only does he conduct his choirs, but he also conducts electricity, in the form of joy, into our hearts.

MALONE

Gareth from *The Office* (47) was a fictional character in the TV show, *The Office*. Gareth later went on to star in three *Pirates of the Caribbean* films as Ragetti, who was played by the actor Mackenzie Crook (also 47). Shiver me timbers – what a talented Gareth!

FROM THE OFFICE

Gareth and the Beanstalk Game

Gareth swapped his star striker for some magic beans which grew into a beautiful beanstalk. But, wait! Is that a pair of golden balls at the top?

Help heroic Gareth choose the right frond to ascend the beanstalk and retrieve the golden balls from the football goose. But choose your path carefully becauseſt

FIFA FO FUM!

Giant Sepp Blatter smells the blood of an English man(ager)!

SOUTHGATE'S
NATIONAL TREASURES

Treasury XI

FORWARDS

MANAGER

GARETH **SOUTHGATE**
MANAGER

SPEED	78
CHARISMA	88
POWER	66
HUGS	95

NT INDEX **90** **100** FOOTBALL SKILLZ

GOALKEEPER

STEPHEN **FRY**
GOALKEEPER

SPEED	16
CHARISMA	72
POWER	98
HUGS	89

NT INDEX **85** **4** FOOTBALL SKILLZ

LEFT BACK

MARY **BERRY**
LEFT BACK

SPEED	84
CHARISMA	14
POWER	17
HUGS	94

NT INDEX **88** **50** FOOTBALL SKILLZ

SIR TREVOR **McDONALD**
CENTRE BACK

SPEED	60
CHARISMA	70
POWER	45
HUGS	67

NT INDEX **89** **76** FOOTBALL SKILLZ

CENTRE BACK

SIR DAVID **ATTENBOROUGH**
CENTRE BACK

SPEED	88
CHARISMA	10
POWER	46
HUGS	32

NT INDEX **100** **66** FOOTBALL SKILLZ

CENTRE BACK

DELIA **SMITH**
RIGHT BACK

SPEED	56
CHARISMA	08
POWER	78
HUGS	12

NT INDEX **79** **89** FOOTBALL SKILLZ

RIGHT BACK

| 11 | 10 | 9 |
| Perry | Moss | Oliver |

| 6 | 7 | 8 |
| Palin | The Queen | Balding |

| 4 | 2 | 3 | 5 |
| Berry | McDonald | Attenbourough | Smith |

| 1 |
| Fry |

LEFT MID

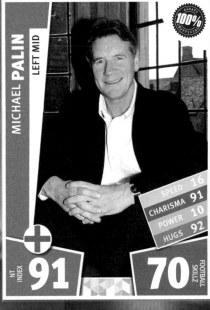

MICHAEL **PALIN** — LEFT MID

| 100% | ALWAYS UNOFFICIAL |

SPEED	16
CHARISMA	91
POWER	10
HUGS	92

NT INDEX **91** **70** FOOTBALL SKILLZ

CENTRE MID

THE **QUEEN** (CAPTAIN) — CENTRE MID

| 100% | ALWAYS UNOFFICIAL |

SPEED	88
CHARISMA	52
POWER	100
HUGS	98

NT INDEX **87** **98** FOOTBALL SKILLZ

RIGHT MID

CLARE **BALDING** — RIGHT MID

| 100% | ALWAYS UNOFFICIAL |

SPEED	68
CHARISMA	70
POWER	44
HUGS	17

NT INDEX **87** **33** FOOTBALL SKILLZ

GRAYSON **PERRY** — LEFT WING

| 100% | ALWAYS UNOFFICIAL |

SPEED	38
CHARISMA	81
POWER	14
HUGS	14

NT INDEX **84** **90** FOOTBALL SKILLZ

LEFT WING

KATE **MOSS** — CENTER FORWARD

| 100% | ALWAYS UNOFFICIAL |

SPEED	100
CHARISMA	10
POWER	70
HUGS	48

NT INDEX **74** **18** FOOTBALL SKILLZ

CENTRE FORWARD

JAMIE **OLIVER** — RIGHT WING

| 100% | ALWAYS UNOFFICIAL |

SPEED	06
CHARISMA	43
POWER	07
HUGS	44

NT INDEX **82** **35** FOOTBALL SKILLZ

RIGHT WING

SOUTHGATE HOLMES

AND THE

Curse of the Speckled Ball

BY
SIR ARTHUR G. SHORE

I n all my years working with the great football detective Southgate Holmes, never have I witnessed a case so strange and so marvellous as the day that football came home to our residence at 4–4–2b Baker Street.

It was late August in the year 2013 that I awoke to find Southgate standing over my bed, with his thumbs tucked into his waistcoat and a profoundly thoughtful expression upon his impressive Roman brow.

'Good Lord, Holmes!' I exclaimed. 'You gave me quite a start!'

'Forgive me for disturbing you at such an early hour, my dear Dr Holland,' said the highly intelligent, yet genuinely approachable man, 'but there is a matter of some importance to which we must attend.'

'Let me guess. Has Mrs Hodgson once again burned the morning muffins?' I offered.

'A fair deduction, given the faint hint of charred bakery produce in the air and the regularity with which our bumbling landlady manages to ruin a perfectly

instance, you are most decidedly wrong. We have a visitor. Come, Holland! Into your track suit! The beautiful game is afoot!'

Truthfully, I was most perplexed by my companion's urgency until, a few moments later, I accompanied him into the sitting room, only to discover none other than the Chairman of the Football Association waiting for us in the window seat.

'Ah, at last,' said the well-paid executive. 'My name is Greg Dyke and this is my personal assistant and treasurer, John Smith.' Mr Dyke gestured to the handsome blond gentleman at his side. 'He's highly efficient and has a great head for figures.'

'Good morning, sirs,' said my supremely wise, yet agreeably down-to-earth partner. 'My name is Southgate Holmes. This is my intimate friend and esteemed colleague Dr Steve Holland. Mr Dyke, might I assume that you won't be requiring any refreshment, given that you have only just breakfasted on a cheese, ham and tomato croissant at the Pret A Manger in Marylebone

'But how on earth could you possibly—' Dyke began, but Southgate interrupted.

'Since your request for this meeting was of the utmost urgency, you would have surely used the quickest mode of transportation to travel the distance from FA headquarters, which, in this case, would be the 9:39 Chiltern Railways Express from Wembley to Marylebone Station. That particular train is made up of only five carriages – none of them a dining car – so you would have had to stop for breakfast along the way. And you most certainly did stop for breakfast; the fresh tomato stain on your left cuff, the cheese crumbs on your lapel, and the small chunk of ham tucked behind your right ear all testify to this fact. And the food item most likely to yield this triumvirate of blemishes would be the Pret A Manger cheese, ham and tomato croissant.'

'How? But—'

'Please, Mr Dyke. Allow me to continue. There are no fewer than eleven branches of Pret between Marylebone Station and these premises. But you must have visited the branch on Marylebone High Street, because that's the branch where Andrzej works. Andrzej makes a mean macchiato, but he has a habit of leaving the croissants on the grill for slightly too long, hence the smell of burning that my colleague Dr Holland remarked upon earlier, when I awoke him.'

The high-earning executive's mouth was agape. 'Good heavens, Mr Holmes,' he said, stunned. 'You really are as good as they say.'

'Why, it's a simple matter of deduction, Mr Dyke,' said Southgate, modestly. 'Plus, you dropped your receipt.' With a raised eyebrow, Holmes handed the man a crumpled Pret A Manger receipt.

Just at that moment, Mr Dyke's blond assistant appeared to make a sudden realisation.

'Goodness! I appear to have left my wallet in Pret. I must retrieve it at once!' Dyke waved the man off absent-mindedly. Southgate showed Mr Smith to the door and turned back to our eminent guest.

'Now, Mr Dyke, how may we help you?'

'Well, since you are the greatest living football detective, I – on behalf of the FA – would like to engage you to solve the biggest mystery of them all: the mystery of why the England men's national team hasn't won a major tournament since the Alf Ramsey era in 1966!'

'I see,' said Holmes, rubbing his beard with a grave, yet pleasantly affable expression. 'Indeed, that is something of a mystery.'

'Whatever we do, whoever we hire, England just can't seem to get the results,' explained Dyke. 'It's almost as if the team is … cursed!'

'Mr Dyke,' retorted the well-tailored master soccer sleuth, 'I can promise you irrefutably that there is no curse. What do I always say in these situations, my dear Holland?'

'Oh! I know this one!' I piped up, enthusiastically. 'Once you eliminate the impossible, whatever remains, no matter how improbable, must be the truth.'

'Well, I was going to say, "curses schmurses", but yes – that, too.'

Something caught Southgate's attention through our bay window and, without warning, he launched himself at Mr Dyke, rugby-tackling him to the floor.

'Good Lord, Southgate!' I exclaimed. 'What on earth do you think you're doing?'

My trusted friend stood up, and plucked something from the wall behind where Greg Dyke had been standing.

'A poisoned blowpipe dart,' he said, examining the missile. 'Clearly someone does not wish us to solve this case!'

Southgate dashed to the window, just in time to see a shadowy, cloaked figure running away from our digs.

'Quick, Holland,' said Holmes, 'we must intercept that man!'

We gave chase, but the cloaked would-be assassin leapt into a taxi and sped off through the busy Baker Street traffic. Holmes, Dyke and I hailed a cab of our own and continued our pursuit, but we lost our quarry just before the Uttoxeter turn-off on the A50.

'Think, think! Who would want to poison the Chairman of the FA?' mused Southgate to himself, as he paced the grass verge near the Uttoxeter Euro Garages services. He sniffed the tip of the dart with his distinguished, highly refined nose. 'A South African variant of oleander,' he remarked. 'Curious …'

'Well, Mr Holmes, since we're so close to England's

training grounds, might I suggest you continue your investigations there?' offered Mr Dyke.

'Indeed. Come, Holland, we must pay a visit to St George's Park at once!'

Later that same morning, the great detective and I arrived at the FA's £105million training facility in Burton upon Trent. As we entered the gates, Holmes cast an eye towards some young street urchins who were knocking about an old-fashioned football – the type that is speckled with black and white panels. We were met by the FA Chairman's dashing blond assistant.

'Find your wallet?' enquired my perceptive partner.

'What? Oh – oh yes,' said the blond man, patting his pocket as he led us to one of no fewer than thirteen outdoor pitches hosted on the site.

'As you can see, we have all the very latest equipment,' boasted Mr Dyke proudly, gesturing to a complex housing more than 25,000 square feet of sporting technology. 'Not to mention some of the best world-class players.'

Southgate surveyed the expensive grounds and the even more expensive players with a quiet, measured intelligence.

'It is indeed an impressive facility, Mr Dyke,' said my sharp-witted, yet amiable companion. 'But there is something missing. If only I could put my finger on it …'

Holmes's attention was drawn by something, but before he could continue, his investigations were interrupted by a young voice.

'Oi, Mister! Pass us the ball.'

We turned to see one of the street urchins – a sandy-haired lad – calling to us from the other side of the gate. The speckled ball the youths had been playing with was rolling towards us.

'Get away!' Mr Dyke's blond assistant told the youngsters, angrily. 'You can't play here! This pitch is for grown-up footballers.'

Without warning, Southgate's aquiline countenance froze, his eyes staring into the middle distance. Seemingly random words began appearing in the air around him, which Holmes pushed around with his hands, his face twitching, as if in fast-forward. I recognised this phenomenon instantly, of course.

MR SMITH

MR DYKE

'What on earth is going on?' enquired our bewildered client. 'Where are those words coming from? Is there something the matter with him?'

'He's perfectly fine,' I explained. 'When Southgate Holmes needs to perform a great feat of deduction, he often retreats into his Crystal Mind Palace.'

'His what?'

'It's a memory technique – an imaginary place called Selhurst Park, where Southgate's mind is free to sift through his memories and focus his cognitive powers.'

Just at that moment, my well-educated and immaculately groomed associate snapped back from his reverie with a start.

'Perhaps you may be able to shed some light on our mystery, Mr Smith,' Holmes said, swirling around to face Mr Dyke's assistant. 'Or, should I call you … Herr Löw!'

In one deft movement, Southgate reached out and pulled off the assistant's floppy blond hair, only to reveal a full head of floppy black hair beneath.

'Joachim Löw! The manager of our arch-footballing rivals, the German national men's team,' exclaimed Dyke.

'Jawohl, it is I,' admitted Löw, hanging his head in shame. 'I admit it. I adopted this disguise in an attempt to sabotage the England team from within, by influencing the FA to waste all its money on expensive equipment and tired, overpaid old players. But might I ask, Mr Holmes, how did you know it was me?'

'It was elementary, really,' said my forward-thinking, yet dependable counterpart. 'My suspicions were first aroused when Mr Dyke described you as "highly efficient" only for you to then claim that you had left your wallet in Pret. It was, of course, all a ruse that allowed you to take your leave and make your assassination attempt from below our window.' Holmes produced the dart from his pocket. 'I presume you obtained the oleander during your visit to Durban Moses Mabhida Stadium for the semi-final of the 2010 South Africa World Cup? Then there was the sausage on the A50. Garlic, marjoram and caraway seeds – the unmistakable recipe for Thuringian Rostbratwurst, a delicacy of your home country, if I'm not mistaken.' Holmes paused. 'Oh, and I also caught you sniffing your fingers after rubbing your own groin.'

'Incredible!' exclaimed Greg Dyke. 'So, we weren't

cursed at all! Just like you said. But wait. That's only half the mystery solved.'

'Here is your answer, Mr Dyke,' said Holmes, picking up the old-fashioned black and white ball.

'I'm afraid I don't follow you, Mr Holmes. No one uses those old things any more. We only use the latest, most expensive balls in our—'

'Not the ball, sir,' interrupted my heroically disruptive friend. 'Rather the young men who kicked it.'

'What? Those young whippersnappers?'

'Those "young whippersnappers", as you call them, are the very solution to your problems, Mr Dyke!' Southgate retorted.

'Ah! Yes! Of course!' said Dyke, as the truth of the matter dawned upon him. 'What you're saying is that we need to invest not only in new technology, but also in the future of English football itself. We need to rejuvenate the game, cultivate grassroots football, uncover a new, fresh generation of young players, perhaps even with a new, young coach at the helm of our under-21s. That's how we solve the mystery of England's floundering international performance. You truly are a genius, Mr Holmes!'

'Well, I was going to suggest getting one of these urchins to take your Pret-stained clothes to the dry-cleaners. But, yes – that as well.'

Just then, the sandy-haired youth trotted up to us.

'Can we 'ave our ball back now please, Mister?'

'Why of course,' said Southgate, handing back the battered old ball with a wise but kindly smile. 'May I ask your name?'

'My name, sir? It's Kane, sir. 'Arry Kane.'

MR HOLLAND

The End

Answers!

GARETH'S BLATTER SPLATTER GAME

Those pesky Sepp Blatter mosquitos were hidden on:

Page 11 Page 15 Page 20 Page 28 Page 32 Page 33

Page 47 Page 49 Page 59 Page 63 Page 70

SOUTHGATE'S SPOT THE BALLS GAME

THE GREAT GARETH HUNT GAME

Answers!

BACK OF THE NET WORDSEARCH

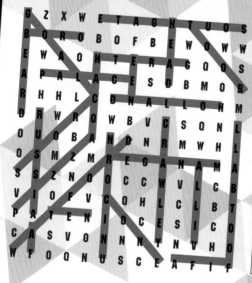

GARETH IS THE BOSS-WORD

GARETH'S WORLD OF CUPS

England = Bone china cup and saucer **Italy** = Espresso cup **Germany** = Stein
France = Breakfast cup (bowl) **Sweden** = IKEA plastic cup **Brazil** = Chimarrao cup

PIZZA HUNT MAZE

GARETH'S A-MAZE-BALLS AMAZING FOOTBALL MAZE

CREDITS

The photostory 'The Penalties of Love' originally appeared in *My Guy* magazine and can be seen in its original 1980s form in *The Best of My Guy* by Frank Hopkinson (ISBN 9781861059796).

Proofreading: Ian Allen

PHOTO CREDITS

Alamy.com: pages 26, 52 & 72 (bottom right), Allstar Picture Library / Alamy Stock Photo; page 38, dpa picture alliance / Alamy Stock Photo; page 40, Rich Gold /Alamy Stock Photo; page 60, ITAR-TASS News Agency / Alamy Stock Photo; page 69 (top left), Everett Collection Inc / Alamy Stock Photo; page 75, Aflo Co. Ltd. / Alamy Stock Photo.

Shutterstock.com: page 3, Dokshin Vlad / Shutterstock.com; page 7, Marco Iacobucci EPP / Shutterstock.com; page 8, Dokshin Vlad / Shutterstock.com; page 10, Featureflash Photo Agency / Shutterstock.com; page 10, Paolo Bona / Shutterstock.com; page 11, Marco Iacobucci EPP / Shutterstock.com; page 12, Marco Iacobucci EPP / Shutterstock.com; page 15, Marco Iacobucci EPP / Shutterstock.com; page 20, Marco Iacobucci EPP / Shutterstock.com; pages 26, 52 & 72 (top left), Marco Iacobucci EPP / Shutterstock.com; pages 26, 52 & 72 (top middle), Featureflash Photo Agency / Shutterstock.com; pages 26, 52 & 72 (top right), Twocoms / Shutterstock.com; pages 26, 52 & 72 (bottom left), Featureflash Photo Agency / Shutterstock.com, pages 26, 52 & 72 (bottom middle), lev radin / Shutterstock.com; page 28, Marco Iacobucci EPP / Shutterstock.com, page 32 (top left), katatonia82 / Shutterstock.com; page 32 (top left), Fabio Diena / Shutterstock.com, page 33 (top left), Mitch Gunn / Shutterstock.com; page 33 (bottom left), katatonia82 / Shutterstock.com; page 33 (bottom left), Ververidis Vasilis / Shutterstock.com; page 39 (bottom right), Marco Iacobucci EPP / Shutterstock.com; page 42, Marco Iacobucci EPP / Shutterstock.com; page 43, Neil Lang / Shutterstock.com; page 44-45, Marco Iacobucci EPP / Shutterstock.com; page 48, I Wei Huang / Shutterstock.com; page 49 (bottom right), kenny1 / Shutterstock.com; pages 53, 73 (bottom right), landmarkmedia / Shutterstock.com; pages 53, 73(top left), Shaun Jeffers / Shutterstock.com; pages 53, 73 (top middle); Featureflash Photo Agency / Shutterstock.com; page 54 (top right), Everett Collection / Shutterstock.com; page 54 (left), Twocoms / Shutterstock.com; page 55 (right), Featureflash Photo Agency / Shutterstock.com; page 55 (top left), steve white photos / Shutterstock.com; page 55 (top right), Everett Collection / Shutterstock.com; page 58 (bottom left), Dokshin Vlad / Shutterstock.com; page 65 (bottom left), Marco Iacobucci EPP / Shutterstock.com; page 66 (top right), Marco Iacobucci EPP / Shutterstock.com; page 68, Featureflash Photo Agency / Shutterstock.com; page 68 (top), imagestockdesign / Shutterstock.com; page 69 (bottom), Featureflash Photo Agency / Shutterstock.com; page 69 (middle), s_bukley / Shutterstock.com; page 71 (bottom left), Marco Iacobucci EPP / Shutterstock.com; page 73 (bottom left), Featureflash Photo Agency / Shutterstock.com; page 73 (bottom middle), Featureflash Photo Agency / Shutterstock.com; page 76 (bottom right), katatonia82 / Shutterstock.com; page 76 (left), Featureflash Photo Agency / Shutterstock.com; page 77, (right) Jaggat Rashidi / Shutterstock.com.